# SILENT CRY

# SILENT CRY

## My Journey Through Domestic Abuse

Mattie Leonard

Tampa, Florida

SILENT CRY:
*My Journey Through Domestic Abuse*

Published by Gatekeeper Press
7853 Gunn Hwy., Suite 209
Tampa, FL 33626
www.GatekeeperPress.com

Copyright © 2022 by Mattie Leonard

All rights reserved. Neither this book, nor any parts within it may be sold or reproduced in any form or by any electronic or mechanical means, including information storage and retrieval systems, without permission in writing from the author. The only exception is by a reviewer, who may quote short excerpts in a review.

The cover design, interior formatting, typesetting, and editorial work for this book are entirely the product of the author. Gatekeeper Press did not participate in and is not responsible for any aspect of these elements.

Library of Congress Control Number: 2022950255

ISBN (paperback): 9781662935527
eISBN: 9781662935534

# CONTENTS

| | |
|---|---|
| DEDICATION | 1 |
| INTRODUCTION | 3 |
| GROWING UP | 9 |
| CHILDHOOD TRAUMA | 15 |
| EARLY ADULT | 21 |
| EARLY MILITARY | 29 |
| CHURCH | 35 |
| MILITARY | 41 |
| DRUGS | 47 |
| CONCLUSION | 51 |
| RESOURCES | 53 |
| BIBLIOGRAPHY | 55 |
| ABOUT THE AUTHOR | 59 |
| OTHER BOOKS BY THE AUTHOR | 61 |

# DEDICATION

Thank you, Lord Jesus, for *Silent Cry: My Journey through Domestic Abuse*.

To my loving family: daughter Shanetta, granddaughter A'Lisa, mother Maria, and father Raymond, who have all been a supportive force in my life. Without them, I would not have made it through my journey of domestic abuse.

Thank you so much. I love each and every one of you. Kisses.

# INTRODUCTION

*Silent Cry* is the heart-wrenching story of my journey through domestic violence and abuse. The National Coalition Against Domestic Violence states that one in five women and one in fourteen men experience sexual violence, physical violence, and/or stalking by an intimate partner during their lifetime. I realized that my past does not define me. You can heal from sexual trauma and abuse. In this book I am breaking the silence and restoring my freedom.

*Silent Cry* helps me to self-reflect on my experiences and moves me toward wholeness. This book will help you transform from survivor to thriver. You will learn how to pick up the pieces of your life, and how strength and resilience allowed me to survive and take back my life. As a result of this and other domestic abuse I suffered, I am determined to overcome the profound effects of trauma—and help others to do the same.

That is where this book comes in—to guide us from our dysfunctional relationship cycles and damaged self-esteem to a life filled with confidence, power, and amazing resilience.

There are four types of intimate partner violence I will talk about in this book. They are sexual violence, stalking, physical violence, and psychological aggression. This book explains my journey through the four types of intimate partner violence or domestic abuse, so brace yourself as you take a walk in my shoes.

Women need to know that they are not traveling alone down these roads of emotional struggle— in the book, I meet them where they are. The main thread throughout, and the place where I feel the most passionate, is helping women understand *why* they have been picking unhealthy relationships, encouraging them to give themselves grace, and supporting them to find the way back to their authentic, wise selves.

Before I go into my journey through domestic abuse, I must explain what it is. Domestic abuse, or domestic violence, is also known as intimate partner violence (IPV). It is any pattern of behavior in any relationship that is used to maintain or gain control and power over a person.

According to K.C. Basile, M.C. Black, M. J. Breiding, J. A. Mercy, L. E. Salzman, and S. G. Smith, in the "National Intimate Partner and Sexual Violence Survey: 2015 Data Brief-Updated Release":

Four types of intimate partner violence are included in this report. These include sexual violence, stalking, physical violence, and psychological aggression.

**Sexual Violence** involves forcing a person to take part in a sexual act when the person does not consent. This can include unwanted sexual contact/touching; sexual harassment at the workplace; incest; exploitation by medical or helping professionals; sexual abuse of the elderly or people with disabilities; prisoner rape; military sexual trauma; as well as the use of technology such as digital photos, videos, apps, and social media, to engage in harassing, unsolicited, or nonconsensual sexual interactions; watching someone in a private act without their knowledge or permission; and showing one's genitals or naked body to others(s) without consent. Gang rape falls into this category.

**Stalking** involves any pattern of repeated and unwanted behavior that is intended to terrorize, annoy, or harass a person. Typical stalking activities include sending unwanted communication through the internet; unwelcome letters or gifts placed on your car, at your home, or sent by mail; video-voyeurism or installing video cameras; repeated telephone calls; surveillance at home, work, and other places that you are known to frequent; and using GPS or other software tracking systems such as spyware on your computer. Stalking usually escalates.

**Physical violence** involves attempting to cause pain and/or physical injury by grabbing, hitting, shoving, kicking, burning, pinching, slapping, choking, hair-pulling, biting, denying medical care, forcing alcohol and/or drug use, use of physical restraints, or using any other physical force. Because of the initial coercion, human trafficking and slavery falls into this category.

**Psychological aggression** involves causing mental or emotional pain or causing fear by intimidation, yelling, or swearing; threatening physical harm to self, person, or children; destruction of pets and property; coercion; ridiculing; "mind games"; treating an adult like a child; using silence to control behavior; or forcing isolation from family, friends, school, regular activities, and/or work.

Abuse in general can also include neglect from a person or self-inflicted neglect and abandonment.

According to K.C. Basile, M.C. Black, M.J. Breiding, J.A. Mercy, L.E. Salzman, and S.G. Smith in the "National Intimate Partner and Sexual Violence Survey: 2015 Data Brief-Updated Release":

> In the United States, the experience of sexual violence, stalking, and intimate partner violence is far too common, with millions of people reporting victimization during their lifetime.

Data from CDC's National Intimate Partner and Sexual Violence Survey (NISVS) indicates:

> About 41% of women and 26% of men experienced contact sexual violence, physical violence, and/or stalking by an intimate partner and reported an intimate partner violence-related impact during their lifetime. Injury, posttraumatic stress disorder (PTSD) symptoms, concern for safety, fear, needing help from law enforcement, and missing at least one day of work are common impacts reported. Over 61 million women and 53 million men have experienced psychological aggression by an intimate partner in their lifetime.

As I walked this journey of life, I faced many traumatic events that shaped my outlook on both other people and myself.

## *One*
# GROWING UP

I was born to a Panamanian woman in Harlem Hospital, in Manhattan, New York City. I lived in a single-family household until my mom met an African American man from Goldsboro, North Carolina. At the age of two, my mother married that man, and he adopted me. As a young girl between two to five years old, I recall my dad telling me I used to walk up to strangers and the bums on the streets of New York City to say hello. I was a happy-go-lucky kid who wouldn't have known danger if it slapped me in the face. Thank God, I had parents to ensure my safety.

As a teen, I was also very naive and always saw the good in people first, never expecting anyone to hurt me or to do me wrong. However, I was a people pleaser, wanting to make people happy by any means necessary. That characteristic would be the start of my spiral downhill.

My dad had joined the military and we went wherever he went. After traveling around the world, he was finally stationed in Fort Hood, Texas. We lived in a town called Killeen. It is a military town thriving off Fort Hood. Killeen is 55 miles (89 km) north of Austin, 125 miles (201 km) southwest of Dallas, and 125 miles (201 km) northeast of San Antonio. According to the 2020 census, its population was 153,095.

I was a very happy child living in a two-parent home. I didn't want for anything. My mom was more of the disciplinarian, while my dad took the time to play games and talk to me.

After a year of being there, my parents decided to get a divorce. My dad moved away, and I stayed with my mom in Killeen. I lost contact with my dad when he moved. I developed typical "daddy abandonment issues."

According to "T. Rodriguez, 5 Things Every Woman Who Grew Up Without a Father Needs to Know":

> Researchers have found that fatherless kids have a higher risk of negative outcomes, including poverty, behavioral problems, and lower educational success. The emotional impact of an absentee dad can be long lasting and has the potential to interfere with healthy relationships in adulthood.

I attended Fairway Middle School. There was no bus service where I lived, so I had to walk to and from school. Luckily, there were plenty of kids on my street who I could walk with. I liked school, especially math. I was outgoing. I played volleyball, ran track, and was a part of the choir at school. I sang soprano and enjoyed everything about it, except my uniform. It was orange and white like the school colors, and I hated it.

I was thirteen years old and in middle school when I had my first experience with sex. It all started one day when a girl named Jaye and I were walking home from school. There were these two boys walking with us. As we passed some newly constructed homes, Jaye had the idea of having sex with one of the boys we were with.

We discussed the matter, and the boy said, "I will have sex with you, if Mattie will have sex with my friend."

She pulled me aside and told me how she really wanted to have sex with him, and could I please have sex with his friend so she could get her way? So, I agreed. I thought, *How bad could it be? A lot of girls were doing it.* We entered the vacant house and went into separate rooms to have sex. It was painful and not at all what I anticipated. After all, this was my first time having sex.

The next day at school, there was a rumor going around saying that I had a bone in my vagina. Some people were teasing me, but others were curious to find out if the rumor was true. I felt like all eyes were glued on me as I struggled to outlive that terrible rumor. After that ordeal I didn't try sex again till I was in high school.

## Sexual Coercion

Sexual coercion can be confusing and deeply distressing. You know what happened wasn't right, but you might not fully understand how or why. You might even believe that they couldn't have assaulted you since you said "yes" in the end. Some coercion tactics include outright threats; guilt-tripping; social pressure; emotional blackmail or manipulation; badgering; denying affection; making you feel bad about yourself; insisting you must follow through; over-the-top affection and compliments; not giving you a chance to say no; and giving you drugs or alcohol with a goal of lowering your inhibitions.

Sexual coercion doesn't have to be by the assailant. In my case, it was a friend—peer pressure at its best. From this incident I have learned that when it comes to anything physical, you absolutely have a voice and do not have to do anything that you don't want to do.

According to J. Litner, PhD, in an article in *Healthline*:

> If you don't really want to have sex but agree because you feel obligated or don't want the other person to get mad, you aren't consenting voluntarily.

According to S. Vulindu in the article "4 Reasons Teenagers Should Wait Until They're Older to Start Having Sex":

> "Don't be pressured into losing your virginity for whatever reason—be it peer pressure, the need for love or the promise of being in a relationship," she says. "The right time is when you're ready. It's a personal decision. You must be emotionally mature enough to handle the consequences of becoming sexually active, so it's a good idea to delay it as long as possible."

\* \* \*

After that experience in the vacant house, I had a reputation as a girl who would have sex, so that peaked a lot of the boys' attention. But I wasn't having it. I shot boys' requests to have sex down left and right. The rumor died down. Finally, I was popular and fit in with the "in" crowd. Later, I would find out that this wasn't a good thing.

*Two*

# CHILDHOOD TRAUMA

We lived on a quiet street that had little to no traffic. Kids played in the road without fear of being ran over. Most kids had keys to their houses because our parents got off work later than we got out of school, so that was our means to get in the house. For a couple of hours, most of the kids, including myself, were unsupervised. My days were blissful for the most part. I would play tag with the children on my street. I would even allow my dog to chase the kids around cars and up trees. They got a kick out of that. I was able to play, do my chores, and finish my homework—all before my mom got home.

One sunny day after school before my mother got home from work, I was playing with the kids up the street. The boys invited me to their playhouse in their backyard. I was so excited and felt like I was accepted. After all, I had no brothers or sisters to play with. So I went, not knowing what was about to happen. Once inside the playhouse, they began touching and fondling me to the point that it was uncomfortable, and I knew it was wrong. I struggled with them and pleaded with them to stop and let me go. But they just laughed and continued their mission. Finally, I was able to break free and run down the street back to my house. I have never been happier to be home and in a safe environment. Who knows what would have happened if I hadn't broken free? I believe that I dodged what could have been a painful experience that day. I never played with those kids again.

## Gang Rape

According to a What-When-How article on *Gang Rape:*

> Gang rape is a serious and greatly understudied form of rape. Gang rape is also sometimes referred to as group rape. Both terms refer to a rape or sexual assault committed by more than one perpetrator against one victim. Most research on gang rape has focused on cases reported to police or incidents in college populations. In general, research has shown that gang rape is less common than rape committed by one offender against one victim, yet more serious in terms of the number and severity of sexual acts suffered by victims.

\* \* \*

I had turned fifteen years old and was attending Killeen High School. Our mascot was a kangaroo. I liked our school color, which was maroon. I was not interested in any school activities like I was in middle school. I just went to school and came home.

It was then that my curiosity about sex began to increase. Not having a father in my life made me seek attention from older guys. Maybe I was looking for a father figure—who knows what motivated my promiscuity.

According to Dr. Seth Myer, author of *The Psychological Root of Promiscuity*:

> Most promiscuous youngsters are promiscuous because they have insufficient supervision or because they have emotional issues (e.g., depression, current or past abuse) that have not been properly identified by parents or treated by professionals.

\* \* \*

One summer day during my sophomore year of high school, I decided to go to my friend's house to surprise him with a visit, only to find out that he wasn't home. I was attracted to this young man's eyes. They were light green, and his tall, muscular build was to die for. He played on the Killeen High School football team and was very popular with the girls at the school. His name was Tee, and he was the first person to perform oral sex on me—on the kitchen floor, I might add. That was mind-blowing as I was only a sophomore in high school and he was two grades ahead of me. Needless to say, I was head over heels for this guy.

His younger brother, Will, was totally the opposite. He was on the chubby side and not attractive at all. When I arrived at their house, Will invited me in to wait for Tee to arrive. We proceeded with small talk as I waited.

Will said, "Have you seen our house? Let me show you around."

I had nothing better to do as I waited; plus, I was eager to see how Tee lived.

As Will showed me the rooms, he was always positioned behind me. I thought nothing of it at the time. When we got to his room, he blocked the entrance and pushed me onto the bed. He began fondling me and pulled down my pants. I fought as hard as I could, but the weight of his body overpowered me. I couldn't believe I was being raped by this guy. When he was finished, I began pulling up my pants and left the room. I held my head down in shame. As I turned the corner, I looked up, and Tee was coming through the door, looking at me with disgust in his eyes.

I just walked by him, not saying a word, and went out the door as fast as I could. I was so humiliated. We never spoke to each other after that day. I could only imagine that he thought I had consensual sex with his brother. I never spoke of the incident to anyone. I was too embarrassed to report it. It was my dirty secret.

## Rape

This incident is not unusual, as it turns out. According to Statista ("U.S. Forcible Rape Cases by State"):

> In 2020 the number of forcible rape cases reported in Texas was 113,509.

\* \* \*

The effects of this incident left me feeling humiliated, angry, degraded, confused, and depressed. The rape wasn't just physically damaging; it was emotionally traumatic as well. It was hard to concentrate in school or to participate in everyday activities. I felt like I would never get over the trauma of the rape. And I didn't for years because I kept silent about the ordeal. I know now that it takes the right emotional attention, care, and support to begin the healing process.

I hated high school with a passion. To get out of school early, I would attend summer school and take classes I needed to graduate. Most kids went to summer school to make up classes they had failed. But I had a different agenda that paid off. I was able to graduate a semester before my class. So, while the other kids were still going to school, I was relaxing at home. Although I didn't have to attend school, I still didn't get my diploma until the school year ended. Being home led me to seek attention and roam the streets, meeting soldiers as I walked around town.

*Three*
# EARLY ADULT

It was on the streets of Killeen where I met one soldier who lived in an apartment complex nearby. I would visit him to pass the time away. On one of my visits to his apartment, we got really comfortable, kissing and fondling each other. We got so far into it that he had taken off my clothes.

After my previous experience, speaking up when something negatively impacted my well-being or sense of self was what I had to do. I knew that I could say "no" and stand my ground. So even though I was half-naked, I said, "I do not want to have sex with you. And I want to leave."

I wasn't prepared for his reaction to my refusal. He got angry, took my clothes, opened the apartment door, and threw them over the balcony. He said, "Now leave."

I was mortified and humiliated. I couldn't believe this was happening to me. *How was I going to get my clothes now?* I was in my panties and bra. I had no choice but to run down the stairs and grab my clothes. Just as I was! I got dressed between parked cars, then walked home. As I took that walk home, I pondered how I could have done things differently. *Maybe I could have said no before I got down to my panties and bra. Maybe I should have stopped before the kissing started.* I don't know, but that half mile seemed like it took forever. You are talking about the walk of shame. Needless to say, I never went to his apartment or talked to that guy again. That was a learning experience for me.

\* \* \*

More light is now being shed on why saying "no" is important. Setting boundaries in life can protect your well-being and provide you with ways to combat certain negatives in a more productive way. But the truth is, when you say "no," you're simply exercising your right to say "no." Because it is a right, not a privilege.

According to T. Robbins:

> Of course, if a hard "no" is still too difficult to say, there are other ways to state it. For instance: "I choose not to," "Not at this time," and "That will not work for me" are all different ways to say "no" that don't feel quite as harsh. Practice turning others down and get more comfortable

in your right to say "no." And remember, it is your right to decide how you spend your time. In the end, remember, it's your right to say "no." It doesn't mean you're exercising some sort of immutable ego trip. It means you're saying "no" because the proposed ask doesn't suit your schedule or beliefs—and that's okay.

* * *

A year later, at the age of sixteen, I met a soldier in the Army at the skating rink in Killeen, Texas. His name was Dimitri, and he was twenty years old. His medium build and a gap between his two front teeth stole my heart. He was so charming and "too good to be true." We would have sex in his car or get a hotel room. We dated for a year before he asked me to marry him. By then I was seventeen and he was twenty-one.

I was so proud that I had married a military man, just like my father. I thought I was set in life. He was the breadwinner and insisted that I didn't work. I was ok with this at first, but having to always ask him for money was a drag, especially when it came to personal items. This was his way of dominating and controlling me.

Quickly into the marriage, I discovered that my husband was abusive. He would pick arguments with me, leave the house for hours on end, and then come back as the nicest person in the world. The honeymoon phase was short, and the tension and violence escalated to physical altercation. I never fought back against him because I didn't know that I could. I thought since he was the man I should just comply. Boy, was I naive. Not only was he abusive, but to make matters worse, he was having extramarital affairs.

The emotional abuse was destroying my self-worth, leading me to anxiety and depression. I felt helpless and alone. I had no sisters or brothers to confide in, and I was too embarrassed to talk to my mother. One day I found myself in another physical altercation over rumors of his affair with a female soldier. The altercation got so bad that I couldn't stand it anymore.

I finally called my mother, who lived in New Mexico at the time. She advised me to seek refuge in a shelter. I left that night. The living arrangements at the shelter were not comfortable. Looking at the building from the outside, you wouldn't know it was a shelter for battered women. There were mothers with children, who naturally made a lot of noise. It took me a long time to fall asleep that night. I went back home after staying one day. I wanted the abuse to end, not the relationship.

A few days later, Dimitri was gone for several hours, and he wouldn't answer my calls. I felt restless, agitated, and indecisive. I couldn't concentrate. I wanted out of the marriage, but mostly I wanted out of my life. I went into my medicine cabinet and I searched drawers to get all the pills I could find in my house. I took them and lay down to die. When my husband finally decided to come home, he found me in a deeply drugged state. He tried to wake me, but I was too drugged up. My speech was slurred, and I was unable to walk without assistance. He knew I was in trouble and took me to the hospital.

I had to get my stomach pumped. The tube they stuck down my throat made me gag something awful. I lay there with tears running down my face as I watched the mixture of blood and undissolved pills leave my stomach through the tube. My throat was sore for days after that ordeal. That was the most awful experience ever, and I wouldn't wish it on my worst enemy.

Five weeks later, I took a pregnancy test, and it was positive. My husband was so excited that he was going to be a father. I, on the other hand, wasn't too happy because the abuse hadn't stopped. In fact, it had gotten worse. But he convinced me to have the baby.

On December 14, 1987, I gave birth to a beautiful baby girl. At birth she had straight, shiny, black hair all over her head. She was fair in complexion and didn't look like either one of us in terms of her shade of skin color. If I hadn't received her immediately after birth, I would have sworn they gave me the wrong child. Life was blissful for a while; the arguments and fights slowed down. We were too preoccupied with our bundle of joy.

My husband changed his MOS (military occupation specialty) to become a cook. We packed up our things and moved to Fort Lee, Virginia, to do his cook training. Once there, the physical violence became more frequent. Our daughter wasn't yet four weeks old when my husband got orders to go to Korea. I was confused, and not even sure if I wanted to stay married at this point. This assignment would give us the much-needed space to figure it out. I decided to call my mother and ask her if I could move in with her. She said I could come to live with her in Albuquerque, New Mexico, while my husband was deployed to Korea. He packed up our stuff and drove us to my mother's apartment.

It took about a month for our daughter's hair to begin to curl up, and her skin became a caramel color. You could see in her facial features the Hispanic side of my mother's family. I was full of life again because of this bundle of joy the Lord had blessed me with and the relief of not being abused anymore.

It was about two months after my husband was gone when I found out that he was AWOL (absent without leave). He had never shown up for his assignment in Korea. After many attempts to make a final decision to leave for good, this was my opportunity. But I felt guilt, insecurity, and concern for my daughter's well-being. All this played a role in my decision-making process. I decided to get a divorce, but I had no clue how to contact him. I contacted a lawyer and told him my dilemma. The lawyer advised me that we could put an ad in the newspaper and petition for a divorce. After a period of time, if there was no response, I could get a divorce through abandonment since I had no clue where he was living.

\* \* \*

Domestic violence is a serious social problem and a national health concern with significant negative impacts on individuals and our communities. The bottom line is that abusive behavior is never acceptable—we deserve to feel valued, respected, and safe.

According to *Psychology Today*:

> Survivors can gradually work to rebuild the self-esteem that was damaged in the relationship.

Developing a non-judgmental support system, practicing self-care, and discussing the experience with a mental health professional can all help survivors in the aftermath of the relationship.

## Four
# EARLY MILITARY

Two years after my divorce, I joined the military. When I finished basic training, I was sent to advanced individual training (AIT). It was there that I met Diablo. My first duty assignment was in Belgium. We were both sent there for a three-year assignment. We were friends and hung out from time to time. But I was the new chick on the block so I had to do my rounds. I frequented the clubs during the night and worked as a systems maintainer during the day. We had to take a duty van to Chièvres Air Force Base where I was working. Every month the low-ranking rotated shifts to be the driver of a duty van transporting workers from SHAPE to Chièvres. At this time, I was living in the barracks on SHAPE, so I needed this transport to get to work.

One day, as I was driving a staff sergeant to Chièvres, he pulled out his penis in the van for me to see. He said, "Touch it."

I just laughed and told him to put it away. I didn't think anything of it at that time. But this was a form of abuse. After all, he was four ranks higher than me, and you would think he would know better.

Another time this same staff sergeant was conducting physical training (PT) in the rain. I was in the front row. He kept making us do push-ups in the rain. My shirt was wet, and you could see my breasts through it. He kept staring at me. Another sergeant noticed what he was doing and made a complaint. His actions fell under the definition of sexual violence. I don't know if anything ever happened to him, but I never saw him again after that day.

When I got promoted to specialist (E-4), the military allowed me to go back to the States to get my daughter and my car. When I got back with my daughter and found a reliable babysitter, Diablo was showing more interest in me. He asked if I wanted to go on a trip with him.

I said, "If you're paying, I will go."

He took me on a trip to Spain, paying for my babysitter to watch my child. A few months later, I married Diablo. We flew to the States and were married by a Justice of the Peace in Virginia with my dad as a witness. When we returned to Belgium, we had a church wedding. We had two singers and a biblical poem on "Love" was read. My dress was white, a mermaid-style gown forming to the shape of my body. I expected my new husband to give me the love and acceptance I couldn't give to myself.

Although he wanted me to get out of the military, I stuck it out. I made it to the rank of sergeant (E-5). It felt like he was in competition with me since we both were in the military, and he was still a specialist (E-4). This put a strain on the marriage constantly. We argued all the time and his jealousy led to physical abuse. After our tour to Belgium, we were stationed at the Pentagon in Washington, DC, and life in our marriage became rough. We fought all the time. This time I fought back, which made the matter escalate. I would wake up the next morning with a headache, fatigue, neck pain, and back pain.

One time I attempted to leave him. He took all my clothes out of the closet and threw them into the fireplace to burn them.

He said, "If you want to leave, you are not taking anything with you." He was holding a fireplace lighter in his hand.

I got the lighter from him and hit him in the head with it. It took a gash of skin out his head. He called the cops on me, and I fled the house before they arrived.

During this time, my husband kept pressuring me to have another child. I was dead set against this idea, especially since he was abusive. Plus, it was rumored that he was having affairs before I got to DC, and that lingered in my head all the time. I was confused about the direction

I wanted to go with this marriage, especially since he was good with my daughter. I never wanted to have another kid, especially not with this man. I'd made this clear from day one. But that was his dream, and I couldn't fulfill that for him.

The marriage was explosive and volatile most days. He would talk down to me in a condescending way, as if I was a child or didn't understand English. I would feel less than. It started to wear down my self-esteem, leading me to feel trapped, worthless, and hopeless. Thank God I was successful in my military career, so I had that strength to hold on to. But that made matters worse because he was not advancing in the military like I was, and that made him degrade me more.

Even our sex was abusive. He would force me to have anal sex all the time. When I would plead for him to stop because it was just too painful and uncomfortable, he would keep going as if I hadn't asked him to stop. I would feel powerless, angry, and sad. But he didn't care how I felt as long as he got what he wanted. I started to develop hatred and deeper resentment towards him. When I would tell him that anal sex was nasty, he would quote a scripture out the Bible: "The marriage bed is undefiled."

I began to regret my life, and depression set in. I didn't dare seek professional help because I had a top-secret clearance, and seeking professional help was frowned upon in the military. It could jeopardize your clearance, causing you to lose it.

I thought every day about leaving him, but I wanted to stay because he was good to my child and treated her like his own. I didn't want my child to grow up fatherless like I did. I thought eventually he would stop abusing me and respect me as his wife because we were going to church. I thought the longer we went to church, the more chance that he would change.

On good days he treated me like a perfect gentleman, opening doors and being nice to me. He would get mad if I opened my own door. But on other days he was a total jerk.

One day, we came home from church, and he was mad at me. He left me sitting in the car for hours and did not open my door. I sat there because I knew it made him angry when I would open my own door. But this day he didn't care. I felt conflicted and didn't know what to do, so I just sat there. Eventually, I figured he wasn't coming back out, and I let myself out the car. These were the type of mind games he would play with me. He was distant and rejecting towards me on most days, and I walked around on eggshells not knowing what would set him off. He was like Dr. Jekyll and Mr. Hyde. Around other people, he treated me like a queen; but behind closed doors, it was the opposite.

When I was stationed in Korea for a year, he eventually found someone else and got her pregnant. That was just the reason I needed to escape, and I filed for divorce. This marriage lasted seven-and-a-half years. I was happy to be free from the abuse and anal rape, but sad to have lost a father for my child.

\* \* \*

According to the article "Onelove: 11 Reasons Why People in Abusive Relationships Can't 'Just Leave'":

> While someone might have used bad judgment by staying in an unhealthy or dangerous situation, it does not mean that they are responsible, or asking, for the abuse perpetrated against them.

Know that you are not alone. Everyone deserves a healthy relationship. At the end of the day, we cannot control anyone else, but we can set boundaries and teach people how to treat us. We don't have to settle for less than what is best for us.

## Five
# CHURCH

After that relationship, I took some time for myself and didn't date.

I decided God himself would have to say, "This is the man for you," before I let anyone into my life again.

My military career was going well as a sergeant (E-5). I was working on Fort Belvoir in Fairfax County, Virginia. I was the training noncommissioned officer (NCO). I loved that job. I had my own office and spent many late nights there doing my work. I was in charge of the company training. I was doing well emotionally and feeling good about myself. I was still living in Virginia and attending a well-known church in the area.

One day while attending church, I saw this six-foot-two-inch-tall, slender man talking to the pastor. His name was Ian. He had naturally curly hair and was a shade darker than I was. He also was a good dresser and presented himself very well. Every Sunday I would look for Ian to come to church. And every Sunday, he did.

One Sunday, he invited me to dinner with him, the pastor, and a couple of other friends. We had a great time talking and eating. When the night was over, Ian mentioned that he had to catch the Metro train to get home. I took that opportunity to offer him a ride home, and he accepted. He lived in Maryland, which was not too far from Virginia.

As we rode home, he began to tell me about his life and the son he had but couldn't see because of a restraining order the child's mother filed against him. I didn't ask him about the child's mother, and he didn't offer more details. In hindsight, I should have inquired more.

He told me that in 1998, he was the man who threatened suicide on a bridge across the Potomac River, snarling traffic on the Capital Beltway for five-and-a-half hours before he jumped. I was astounded because I had heard about the incident but could not imagine that it was him. Ian said that he was depressed about not being able to see his child and was suicidal. I had empathy for him because many times in my life I thought about suicide and knew how easy it was for someone to get into that mind frame. I didn't judge him but listened with compassion.

Ian expressed that he was doing better now and shared how God had helped him heal from that ordeal.

I thought, *Wow, a godly man too.* And it showed as I observed him Sunday after Sunday at church. He was very outgoing, and people liked him. They encouraged us to date. I figured if people were recommending him to me, then he must be a good guy.

I was hesitant at first. But after about a month, we began to date. He was so loving and caring. He would bring me flowers and toys for my daughter. We hit it off great. We began to have sex after about a month of dating. He never pressured me to have sex; it just came naturally. I liked that about him. Ian was so romantic and such a gentleman. Nothing like my previous relationships.

But there was one red flag I missed. He would call me several times a day as if he had no job, sometimes back-to-back when I didn't answer his calls. He would have a conversation with my answering machine when I didn't answer. It was getting to be a bit annoying. He would show up at my apartment unannounced with flowers or a gift. The gifts I appreciated—but coming unannounced I didn't like. He began to seem too clingy for my liking.

If I was not reachable, he would start accusing me of being with someone else, always asking where I was and who I was with. But Ian was never violent towards me, so I overlooked his needy ways. I actually loved the attention he was giving me.

However, after several months it got to be annoying, and it got even worse when I got pregnant. By now he knew where I frequented and would come looking for me at those places. Sometimes he would come in, but other times he would leave something on my car to let me know he was there. I thought that was strange and started to become a bit wary. His jealousy took a turn for the worst, and he began threatening me.

One time he went to my daughter's school. That was the last straw for me. He had no business at my daughter's school, so I called the police to let them know about his behavior and how I was starting to fear for my life. They told me I was being stalked and advised me to keep an accurate journal or log of all incidents connected to the stalking. He started leaving messages saying if he couldn't have me, no one could. I kept any evidence received from him such as text messages, voicemails, letters, packages, and emails.

One day when I wasn't home, my neighbors witnessed him getting a ladder off of a nearby utility truck, climbing up onto my balcony, throwing my dog off the balcony, and leaving with my dog. I was frightened for my daughter, myself, and my unborn child. I decided to have an abortion because I wanted nothing to do with this guy.

I tried to avoid Ian at all costs. I even stopped going to the church where we met. When he found out that I had an abortion, he became angrier, and the level of stalking increased. He left a message saying, "You took one of mine; now I have to take one of yours." I didn't know what that meant, but I wasn't willing to find out. I went to the military personnel and requested a transfer overseas to get away from him. I knew that if I went anywhere in the United States, Ian would follow me. They said, "We have an assignment in Turkey." I didn't care where it was just as long as it was far away. The transfer was granted, and we prepared to leave.

Before I left for Turkey, Ian was apprehended and convicted of stalking me. He served eighteen months in jail for the stalking charge.

## Stalking

According to National Center for Injury Prevention and Control, Division of Violence Prevention:

> Stalking is a public health problem that affects millions of people in the United States. Stalking involves a perpetrator's use of a pattern of harassing or threatening tactics that are both unwanted and cause fear or safety concerns in a victim. The National Intimate Partner and Sexual Violence Survey (NISVS) reports that about 1 in 3 women and 1 in 6 men have been stalked at some point in their lives.

## Six
# MILITARY

I was stationed in a town called Izmir in Turkey. I was able to take my daughter with me on this tour. While in Turkey, I mingled with the Turkish people.

Turkey is a transcontinental country located mainly on the Anatolian Peninsula in Western Asia, with a small portion on the Balkan Peninsula in Southeast Europe. It shares borders with the Black Sea to the north; Georgia to the northeast; Armenia, Azerbaijan, and Iran to the east; Iraq to the southeast; Syria and the Mediterranean Sea to the south; the Aegean Sea to the west; and Greece and Bulgaria to the northwest. I visited several towns in Turkey, including Bodrum, which overlooked the Aegean Sea, and Kusadasi, which was the largest resort town with lovely beaches.

One day the military travel agency coordinated a trip to visit the Seven Churches of Asia as stated in the Book of Revelation in the Bible. I was able to see the remains of churches located in Turkey. The Seven Churches of Asia include: Ephesus, Smyrna, Pergamum, Thyatira, Sardis, Philadelphia, and Laodicea. Jesus Christ instructed John of Patmos to write about what he observed at these churches.

While in Turkey, I had a Turkish friend who I went everywhere with. Wherever you saw her, you saw me. She worked at the dry cleaner on NATO where I worked. I started learning Turkish and became somewhat fluent in the language. Let's just say that I could say a few sentences to get me around. Furniture was cheap there, and you could get anything custom-made. I bought a wrought-iron canopy bed; a complete dining room set, including the buffet with mirror; and a wrought-iron figurine stand. I collected black art statues. I had a maid who would come clean my house once a week for twenty dollars, and she was thorough in her cleaning.

The clubs were the highlight of the town. One club I went to had foam and bubbles in the entire room. That was pretty interesting.

One night me and my friend went to this Turkish club. I ordered a drink and left it at the bar to go dance. When I came back, I began drinking my drink. A few minutes later I had a sense of euphoria, increased energy, and a heightened sense of promiscuity. I was feeling sensual and down for anything. I felt like everyone I came across was my friend. I ended up going home with this girl I was dancing with. But my friend was my saving grace. She ensured that nothing bad happened to me. The next day she told me that we ate breakfast then caught a cab and went home. I didn't remember much of anything. All I knew was that I woke up at home. I later found out that my drink was probably laced with ecstasy.

\* \* \*

The lines of consent may be blurred while under the influence and can cause an increased chance of sexual assault. I learned to never leave your drink unattended. After all, the consequences can be your demise.

\* \* \*

After my eighteen-month tour in Turkey was over, I was stationed in Fort Gordon, Georgia, for four years. There I was the tasking NCO for the brigade, responsible for assigning tasks to soldiers. During the four years we were there, my daughter was able to graduate from high school.

One day, the White House recruiting team came to Fort Gordon looking for likely candidate to recruit. My MOS as a microwave system maintainer was one of the job titles they were looking for. I submitted my packet and was accepted.

The military transferred me to DC to begin a job at the White House. Before I left, I was promoted to staff sergeant (E-6). DC was too expensive to live in, so I purchased a townhouse in Oxon Hill, Maryland. By then I had two Rottweilers and needed a place with a fenced-in yard.

After about a year working as wideband radio technician (WRT), I was promoted to sergeant first class (E-7), and I was given the role of noncommissioned officer in charge (NCOIC) of the White House Situation Room (WHSR). I oversaw eight people: two civilians, three Air Force soldiers, two Navy soldiers, and one Army soldier. My career was going well. I traveled with the president, vice president, and first lady to locations such as Texas, Louisiana, Georgia, Alabama, Honduras, and Kazakhstan, to name just a few. On my off time, I was taking hand dancing lessons and frequenting clubs.

One day the police came to my house to tell me that I was a possible victim of up skirting.

I said, "What is up skirting?"

They proceeded to tell me that up skirting involves taking a picture under a person's clothing without them knowing with the intent of viewing their genitals or buttocks for sexual gratification or to cause upset to the victim. They told me that while they had been monitoring a man, they conducted a search of his premises and confiscated a video camera that had a video of me washing my car. The way they found me was because he videotaped my license plate number on my car while he filmed up my skirt as I washed my car.

I felt humiliated and violated when I saw the video. He had filmed me down my shirt and up my skirt at different angles. I couldn't believe that this filming was going on without my knowledge. They asked me if I had seen anything suspicious that day. But I hadn't. I just remembered a guy coming up to me trying to sell CDs and he put the CD holder on the ground by my foot. That wasn't suspicious to me. The police asked me if I wanted to press charges, and I said yes.

We ended up going to court, and this man's wife sat right by his side. Unfortunately, the case was thrown out on a technicality. The police forgot to label the CD that the video was on, and his lawyer said that there was no proof that it was a video from his videorecorder. I was angry that I had wasted my time going to court.

* * *

According to Tes Safeguarding:

> On 12 April 2019, a new law banning the invasive practice came into force across England and Wales and offenders can now be arrested and sent to prison. The criminal offence of 'up skirting' was created under the Voyeurism Act when it received Royal Assent in February 2019. Police and prosecutors have now updated their guidance to ensure the law is properly enforced—with offenders facing up to two years in jail and being placed on the sex offenders' register. The law was changed following campaigning from Gina Martin and other victims, MPs and charities who worked closely with Ministers to create the new law and protect more victims.

*Seven*
# DRUGS

I stayed at the White House a total of five years. I ended up retiring with an injured back and was put on opiates. That was the beginning of my drug addiction. When I retired, I moved back to Killeen, Texas, to be closer to my mom. But the pain in my back didn't subside, and I couldn't find a doctor there who would give me pain pills. My drug addiction progressed to street drugs.

I continued to look for people that I could get my drug of choice from. I asked this guy named JC, who I had known for about a year. He was in my peer support group at the VA hospital. I knew JC smoked weed on the regular, so I figured he might know a connection to where I could get wet, which is a tobacco or marijuana cigarette dipped in embalming fluid mixed with PCP.

He said he was going to Houston and could get wet for me, but there was one stipulation. I would have to use it at his house so that I wasn't alone in case anything happened. I felt that after knowing him for a year and visiting his house on several occasions, he could be trusted, so I agreed. I just wanted the fix, and plus, it was going to be New Year's at midnight, and I didn't want to be alone.

JC picked me up in his blue Cadillac, and we arrived at his apartment. JC was living in a senior community and had a two-bedroom apartment. He rolled a joint, and we shared it, but I wanted my wet. He got the wet from his refrigerator. There were two wrapped in aluminum foil. He placed them on the table. I immediately opened the wrapping. I lit one and put the other one in my purse while he was pulling the steaks out the refrigerator. Finally, he had given the wet to me, and I was a happy camper.

He tried to ration it to me, went into my purse, and took the other one back from me when I wasn't looking. When I realized it was gone, I overlooked it because I knew I was going to smoke it later anyway. But it made me furious that he had gone through my purse to retrieve it.

He cooked dinner while I watched TV. In between the cooking, we managed to smoke three more joints before I asked for something more comfortable to wear. JC gave me one of his jerseys to wear. There I was with a jersey top on with no pants. By now he had invited me to stay over in his extra room. I agreed since I was having so much fun listening to music, watching TV, doing my wet, and smoking joints.

While I was watching TV and he was cooking, he offered to smoke another joint, and I lost some time. In other words, I had blacked out, but I didn't know this until he told me he had to take me outside to get me some air to bring me back to consciousness. I couldn't walk so well. I recall saying something like, "I can't walk." But it was a blur. I just didn't clearly recall.

JC smoked another joint, but I didn't because now I was craving wet again, so he finally gave me the second one. I was so excited. I was still mad that he'd taken it out of my purse to control when I could have it. I smoked it and blacked out again. This time when I came to, he was lying behind me and raping me. I asked him what he was doing, and he stopped. He said he thought I had overdosed, and he thought he was going to have to take me to the hospital.

I saw the bowl of water and washcloth he said he was using to cool me down. But I guess somehow while cooling me down, he got turned on and decided to rape me while I was under the influence of my blackout state. How sickening—it's like having sex with a dead person. But I was still so out of it, I was in no position to argue or go home. So, I stayed and pretended that nothing had happened.

When he finally took me home the following morning, the reality of what had happened set in. I had been raped by a so-called friend. The anger and shame became prevalent. I tried to play back the account that took place. I asked myself, *did I consent and didn't remember it? Was it actually rape?*

The next day I went to the VA to talk to my peer support counselor. JC and I had the same peer support counselor at the VA hospital. I told the counselor what had happened and that I couldn't be his patient any longer because I was fearful that I might see JC again. He wasn't too happy that I wasn't going to come back to him for counseling, but he understood. I never saw JC after that assault.

The effects of this incident left me feeling scarred and fearful of so-called friends from then on. I questioned people motives frequently. My trust in people had diminished. In cases like this with a drug-related sexual assault, survivors often blame themselves. I had to remember I was not to blame. I am the only one allowed to make choices for my body. Using drugs or alcohol is never an excuse for assault and does not mean that it was my fault.

# CONCLUSION

The first thing you must determine if you are being abused is whether it is sexual violence, stalking, physical violence, or psychological aggression. No one deserves this behavior. Speak up, get out of the situation, and seek healing.

If I were to dwell upon the negative incidents in my life, I would be a depressed person. In fact, I was depressed for years because I kept silent and dealt with my grief internally. I felt that no one should know the dirty secrets of my life.

But healing from domestic abuse is imperative. It helps to have a therapist or people you can talk to on a regular basis. Talking about it not only helps you make sense of what you're experiencing but also provides support, validation, and resources from someone who has been through the same things you've been through. The benefit of talking to someone is having an ear to listen and someone to let you know that you are not alone. If you are not comfortable with a particular person, you can use a confidential hotline to connect with a professional in the field. The bottom line is knowing your worth, value, and setting boundaries. You are the only one who can teach people how to treat you. Remember that hurt people hurt people.

# RESOURCES

## Crisis Support Service
## Sexual Assault and Harassment

National Sexual Assault Hotline: a service of RAINN
Online chat hotline
Spanish online chat hotline
Telephone hotline: 800-656-HOPE (4673)

National Street Harassment Hotline: a service of Stop Street Harassment
Online chat hotline
Telephone hotline: 855.897.5910

DoD Safe Helpline: a service for members of the U.S. military and their families, operated by RAINN for the Department of Defense
Online chat hotline
Telephone hotline: 877.995.5247

## Domestic and Dating Violence

National Domestic Violence Hotline
Online chat hotline
Telephone hotline: 800.799.SAFE (7233)

Love is Respect: a service of the National Domestic Violence Hotline
Online chat hotline
Telephone hotline: 866.331.9474

# BIBLIOGRAPHY

Basile, K.C., Black, M.C., Breiding, M.J., Mercy, J.A., Salzman, L.E., & Smith, S.G. (2018). The national intimate partner and sexual violence survey: 2015 data brief- updated release. Atlanta: National Center for Injury Prevention and Control Centers for Disease Control and Prevention. *https://www.cdc.gov/violenceprevention/datasources/nisvs/summaryreports.html/*.

CDC Centers for Disease Control and Prevention. (2022) Fast Facts: Preventing Intimate Partner Violence. Retrieved from https://www.cdc.gov/violenceprevention/intimatepartnerviolence/fastfact.html/

Dr. Seth Myers. (2013, August 8). The Psychological Root of Promiscuity. Retrieved from *https://www.eharmony.com/dating-advice/dating/the-psychological-root-of-promiscuity/*.

Litner, J., PhD. (2020) Healthline: Sexual Health. Retrieved from *https://www.healthline.com/health/sexual-coercion*.

National Center for Injury Prevention and Control, Division of Violence Prevention. (2022) Fast Facts: Preventing Stalking. Retrieved from *https://www.cdc.gov/violenceprevention/intimatepartnerviolence/stalking/fastfact.html/*

Onelove. (n.d.). 11 Reasons Why People in Abusive Relationships Can't "Just Leave". Retrieved from *https://www.joinonelove.org/learn/why_leaving_abuse_is_hard/*.

*Psychology Today.* (n.d.). Domestic Violence: Spousal Abuse, intimate Partner Violence. Retrieved from *https://www.psychologytoday.com/us/basics/domestic-violence*

Robbins, T. (n.d.). You have the right to say "No". Retrieved from *https://www.tonyrobbins.com/mind-meaning/the-power-of-no/#:~:text=But%20the%20truoh%20is%2C%20when,a%20right%2C%20not%20a%20privilege.*

Rodriguez, T. (2016, September 26). 5 Things Every Woman Who Grew Up Without a Father Needs to Know. Retrieved from

*https://www.womansday.com/relationships/family-friends/q-and-a/a56444/fatherless-daughters/*.

Statista. (2020). U.S. Forcible Rape Cases by State. Retrieved from

*https://www.statista.com/search/?q=forcible+rape+cases+in+the+us+by+state&Search=&qKat=search&newSearch=true&p=1*

Tes Safeguarding. (2019, August 15). Up skirting: What do you need to know? *https://www.educare.co.uk/news/upskirting-what-do-you-need-to-know.*

What-When-How (n.d.). Gang Rape. Retrieved from *http://what-when-how.com/interpersonal-violence/gang-rape/*.

Vulindu, S. (2019). DRUM: 4 reasons teenagers should wait until they're older to start having sex. Retrieved from *https://www.news24.com/drum/advice/4-reasons-teenagers-should-wait-until-theyre-older-to-start-having-sex-20191101*.

# ABOUT THE AUTHOR

**Marianela Leonard** rose through the ranks of the U.S. Army to Sergeant First Class, SFC, E-7 before retiring after twenty years of service. During her last five years in the military, she worked in the White House Situation Room. She earned a BA in Information System Management (IFSM) and an MBA from National-Louis University (NLU) in Illinois. Marianela is a resident of Killeen, Texas. She is a daughter, mother, grandmother, and author. When she is not writing, you can find her doing service work at Narcotics Anonymous (NA), taking swing dance classes, walking her dogs, and enjoying her backyard oasis.

# OTHER BOOKS BY THE AUTHOR

*Building Me Back Brick by Brick* brings awareness to addiction through my own life experiences and has been written to help others in their recovery process. Life on life's terms happens, and I learned that you have to go through the struggles instead of hiding behind drugs, pills, alcohol, and sex. This book will show you mentally, physically, spiritually, and emotionally how to deal and how not to deal with your addiction.

### Join Mattie Author Page on Facebook
*Mattie Leonard*

### Join Mattie's Web Page
*https://mattieleonard.com*

www.ingramcontent.com/pod-product-compliance
Lightning Source LLC
LaVergne TN
LVHW051219070526
838200LV00064B/4972